The Unification Church

STUDIES IN CONTEMPORARY RELIGIONS

Volumes in Print:

The Church of Scientology
by J. Gordon Melton

The Unification Church
by Massimo Introvigne

Volumes in Preparation:

*Soka Gakkai:
From Lay Movement to Religion*
by Karel Dobbelaere

Osho Rajneesh
by Judith M. Coney

The Children of God—The Family
by J. Gordon Melton

The Theosophical Society
by James A. Santucci

Additional volumes to follow.

The Unification Church

Massimo Introvigne

STUDIES IN CONTEMPORARY RELIGIONS

Massimo Introvigne, Series Editor

Signature Books
in cooperation with CESNUR
(Center for Studies on New Religions)

Cover design by Ron Stucki

© 2000 Elle Di Ci, Leumann (Torino), Italy.
This edition is published by arrangement with the copy-
right holder.

Published in the United States of America by Signature
Books. Signature Books is a registered trademark of
Signature Books, Inc.

All photographs appear courtesy HSA-UWC New Future
Photo.

LIBRARY OF CONGRESS CATALOGING-IN-PUBLICATION DATA
Introvigne, Massimo.
    [Chiesa dell'unificazione. English}
    The Unification Church / Massimo Introvigne.
      p. cm. — (Studies in contemporary religions ; 2)
    Includes bibliographical references (p.).
    ISBN 1-56085-145-7 (paper)
    1. Unification Church—History. 2. Unification
    Church—Doctrines. I. Title. II. Series.

  BX9750.S43 I58 2000
  289.9'6—dc21

                                        00-033885

Contents

1.

Sources

The Unification Church founded by the Reverend Sun Myung Moon is one of the religious organizations most often defined today as a cult. Nevertheless, information about the church available to the general public, as well as to those specifically interested in new religious movements, is not always precise or complete. For several reasons, sensational literature and the popular media often play a pre-eminent role in spreading arbitrary and false information about the Unification movement. The contents of this book briefly discuss the history, doctrine, and practices of the Unification Church. Some authors use the term "Unificationism" to describe a movement greater than the Unification Church. Included in this expression are people or groups diversely inspired by the Unification Church but formally not part of it; others describe, by using the term "Unificationism," the general philosophy of the movement. In this book the term "Unificationism" indicates the doctrine and activity of the Unification Church.

Before commencing our exposition, it would be appropriate to illustrate, even if synthetically, the different approaches that have been used to study Unificationism. The bibliography on the church and its founder is vast, and may be found mostly in Japanese, Korean, and English. It is important, I believe, to distinguish among the different sources to provide a comprehensive look at Unificationism, beginning with a division of works into three principal groups—primary, scholarly, and controversial —which can be differentiated because of their style and objectives.

Primary sources consist of manuals and writings of the Unification Church, the most important being the *Divine Principle*.[1] Following Jin-choon Kim, dean of the College of Theology at Sun Moon University in Korea, we may identify seven periods in the formative history of the *Divine Principle*:

1. Revelations received by Rev. Moon (but not written or taught to others) between April 17, 1935, and August 15, 1945.

2. The early ministry of Rev. Moon, from August 15, 1945, to May 10, 1952 (with a number of revelations taught to disciples, but no written text).

3. The use of a first handwritten manuscript, *Wolli Wonbon* ("Original Text of the Divine Principle"), completed on May 10, 1952, and used until August 15, 1957.

4. The use of *Wolli Haesul* as a standard text ("Explanation of the Divine Principle"), prepared by Hyo Won Eu, based on both *Wolli Wonbon* and Rev. Moon's sermons. It was published on August 15, 1957, and used until May 1, 1966.

5. The use of *Wolli Kangron* as a standard text ("Exposition of the Divine Principle"), prepared by Hyo Won Eu and adding new material from Rev. Moon's sermons. It was published on May 1, 1996, and used until September 30, 1994.

6. The use of a color-coded version of *Wolli Kangron*, published on September 30, 1994, the primary standard reference until November 1, 1997.

7. The period beginning November 1, 1997, when Rev. Moon began the tradition of *Hoon Dok Hae*, including a daily study session in the morning, for which excerpts from his sermons were prepared, and regarded as "complementary expression of the Completed Testament Word," together with the *Wolli Kangron*.[2]

Numerous translations and versions of the *Divine Principle* have been made. Added to this is a collection of speeches by Rev. Moon.[3] There are many different doctrinal publications, among which at least two may be considered essential: *Unification Theology* written by Dr. Young Oon Kim (an authoritative but unofficial text[4]) and a work that is philosophical in character, *Explaining Unification Thought*, written by the Korean Unificationist Sang Hun Lee.[5] Up until a few years ago there was, among the church's required readings, an important manual on communism, *The End of Communism*, which was also the work of Sang Hun Lee.[6] After his death, Lee has continued to speak, according to Unificationists, from the spirit world, and such messages are read with great interest by many church members.[7] In fact, "Lee's book has nearly scriptural status. Rev. Moon endorsed it as suitable for *Hoon Dok Hoe* readings."[8]

Other relevant primary sources include:

1. The autobiographies of personalities in the Unification Movement such as that of Mose Durst,[9] president of the Unification Church in the United States up to 1987, or of Chong Goo Park[10] (called Tiger Park) who died in 1982 and whose diary was published posthumously; and also that of Henri Blanchard,[11] the first French member and president of the Unification Church in France up to 1994.

2. Manuals and rituals set up for members of the Unification Church.[12]

3. Michael Breen's book, *Sun Myung Moon: The Early Years 1920-53*, well documented and exhaustively researched. He describes himself as a lapsed member of the Unification Church.[13]

4. Internet Websites have become a source of current speeches as well as a historical archive of speeches of Rev. Moon and elder Unificationists. Activities of the many organizations initiated by Rev. Moon and their activities and to a lesser extent news are provided by a series of mostly unofficial Websites, both official (such as the Completed Testament News http://family.tongil. or.kr/ctnews) and unofficial (e.g., www.unification.net; www.tparents.org; www.ettl.co.at/uc).

5. Finally, the numerous weekly or monthly public magazines published by the Unification Church and connected organizations, in different languages (e.g., the *Unification News*), as well as those reserved for members (e.g., *Today's World, The European*, or *Tongil Sae Gye* in Korean) or for scholars (*Journal of Unification Studies*).

Scholarly studies of the Unification Church are generally the work of sociologists of religion interested in Unificationism, though more as a social movement and not in its theology and beliefs. One of the first studies of this type, *The Doomsday Cult,* by John Lofland,[14] resulted from field research conducted among members of the first Unification mission in the United States in the 1960s. Eileen Barker, of the London School of Economics, has published a portion of her observations, which she recorded over a period of time with members, in a study dedicated principally to the reasons why many young people decided to follow Unificationism.[15] Another seminal work is the history of the Unification Church in the United States by David G. Bromley and Anson D. Shupe, Jr.,[16] both well-known sociologists in the field of new religious movements. A similar work has been authored in England by George Chryssides.[17] Among theologians interested in the Unification Church was the late Jesuit professor and sociologist Joseph H. Fichter. One of his first articles on the subject, somewhat favorable to Unificationism, was published in 1979 in the magazine *America* and aroused some controversy.[18]

Almost all works in this category include interesting analyses of the structure of the Unification Church as a social group,[19] but they often miss the theological aspects of the movement. Major attention to these themes of Unificationism, intended as a "world view" more than a religion as such, came from Catholic priest Sebastian A. Matczak, in an extensive study taken from an ecumenical perspective.[20] The Unification Church itself was somewhat happy to be the object of sociological studies, and eventually promoted seminars and publications on new religions.[21]

Controversial literature constitutes the third group of publications. In this group the autobiographical testimonies of ex-Unificationists, who have abandoned their previous faith, comprise the major part. Among the most notable examples is the early book by Deanna Durham.[22] In 1998 Rev. Moon's former daughter-in-law, Nansook Hong, authored one of the most comprehensive apostate indictments of the church to date.[23] More or less violent attacks against the Unification Church have been published mostly in the United States by members of many different Evangelical organizations.[24] On the Catholic side, controversial works are less numerous—the writings of French Catholic priest Pierre Le Cabellec could be cited.[25]

Besides this controversial literature from the religious side, there exists a long list of works particularly violent in nature which attack the Unification Church from the perspective of secular humanism or political criticism, examining its economic activities and political stance. The classic example of this type of literature is the (rather gossipy) 1986 work of French journalist Jean François Boyer[26] in which he denounced the movement's anti-Communist activities and all its collaborators, rather than analyzing the religious aspect of the phenomenon.

There is some extensive literature available, enriched by the inclusion of several court cases, that took place mostly in the United States, detailing accusations of "brainwashing" brought against the Unification Church by the parents of young adherents.[27] Eventually, some of these parents organized "deprogrammings," in which the followers of the church were kidnapped and subjected to a particular treatment to persuade them to abandon Unificationism. The father of "deprogramming," Ted Patrick, has related his experience in a volume written in collaboration with Tom Dulack, *Let Our Children Go*.[28]

In general, the anti-cult literature is mostly found in

bulletins and magazines, many of which are poorly produced. By the 1980s this had already reached such proportions as to make it necessary to use bibliographic tools in order to study such literature.[29]

2.

History

The history of the Unification Church is inseparable from that of its founder, whose given name was Yong Myung Moon which was changed when he was twenty-five to Sun Myung Moon. Yong Myung Moon was born in Cheong-Ju, a village now situated in North Korea, on January 6, 1920.[1] He was the fifth of eight children born to a couple who converted to the Presbyterian church when young Moon was ten years old. According to official biographies, Jesus Christ appeared to Yong Myung Moon when he was sixteen, revealing that he had chosen him for a special mission. However, at that time Yong Moon did not tell anyone about this revelation which was the first of many he received. In 1938 he left his native village for Seoul, capital of Korea, where he enrolled in a course in technology. Korea in 1941 was still under Japanese occupation, and Moon went to Tokyo to study engineering at Waseda University. In 1943, in the midst of the Second World War, he returned to Korea where he worked in a construction company. He also became involved in a movement fighting for Korean independence against the Japanese. He was discovered, arrested, and imprisoned for four months by the Japanese political police.

At the end of the war, during a period of great religious fervor in Korea, Sun Myung Moon decided to dedicate himself to preaching full time. He married Sun Kil Choi, a fervent Christian, in November 1943.[2] In June 1946, shortly after the birth of his first son, Sung Jin (Moon),[3] he declared that he had received a revelation which commanded him to go to Pyongyang, a city situated in Communist North Korea. He left for North Korea while his wife remained in Seoul. Reunited again in Pusan in November 1952, Mrs. Moon found that being a pastor's wife after surviving the pain of separation for six years was too difficult to bear. Unable to accept her husband's commitment to his calling, she divorced him.[4] Today Sun Kil Choi and Sung Jin Moon are both members of the Unification Church and both have received the "Blessing."[5] Sung Jin Moon was "blessed" in the early 1970s; his mother, Sun Kil Choi, was "blessed" on June 13, 1998.

In July 1946 Rev. Moon founded an independent Christian church called Kwang-ya, characterized by a strong charismatic enthusiasm. It appears that married women were advised to live in chastity until their marriage was "blessed" by Rev. Moon.[6] This new group quickly attracted the hostility of Communist authorities and its leader was arrested in 1946 and again in 1948. He was tried and condemned to five years of hard labor in a prison camp in Hung-Nam. After two and a half years of imprisonment, Rev. Moon and two of his disciples, making use of the advance of American troops during the Korean War, were able to reach the South. In 1951 Rev. Moon recommenced preaching in a simple hut made of mud and cardboard in a refugee camp in Pusan.

After having developed the first nucleus of his doctrine—known as the *Divine Principle*—Rev. Moon left Pusan and went to Seoul, where on May 1, 1954, he founded the Holy Spirit Association for the Unification of World Christianity, later known as the Unification Church. In Seoul the young movement was especially successful in converting young female students and professors from Ewha University, a well-known Christian school. Alarmed, university authorities sent a group to study and prepare a report on Unificationism. On this occasion one of the young women in the group, the theologian Young Oon Kim, converted to Unificationism and played an important role until her death in 1990.

In 1955 the first Korean edition of the *Divine Principle* was distributed to members of the movement. As the movement grew, so did opposition, and in 1955 Rev. Moon was again arrested. According to Unification biographies, he was accused of evading military service, even though at the time of conscription he had been imprisoned in Hung Nam. Other works claim the church was accused of wrongdoing and that it practiced sex rituals.[7] Nevertheless, on October 4, 1955, Rev. Moon was absolved of all accusations and freed. A few days later the church acquired a Buddhist temple at Chong-Padong, an area in Seoul, which became its headquarters. From that time on, Unificationism became a national phenomenon; by the end of 1955, there were already thirty Unification centers throughout South Korea. In 1960 the marriage between Rev. Moon and his present wife, Hak Ja Han, took place. Unificationists—who regard the marriage as having great theological significance—believe that this event was a major development in the life of the founder and in the history of the church.

In the meantime, on June 16, 1958, the first Unification Church missionary, Sang Ik-Choi, left Korea for Japan, one of the countries where Unificationism would later enjoy its great success. Other missionaries eventually went to the United States, among whom was Yun Soo Lim, called Onni (Korean for "elder sister"). She came to the U.S. with Sang Ik-Choi after he left Japan, and was later "blessed" (married) to Doctor Mose Durst, her spiritual child (i.e., she had converted him); together they took charge of the "Oakland family" in California. This was the most important center of proselytism for the Unification Church. The couple remained in California until May 1980, when Durst was nominated to be president of the Unification Church of the U.S.A. and went to live in New York.

Towards the mid-1960s, many young people who had joined the church in the United States were sent back to their countries of origin to spread Unificationism in Europe. The first small groups developed in Italy, Germany, Austria, and Spain. In France the first missionary, Reiner Vincenz, arrived in Paris in February 1966. The first member, Henri Blanchard, joined the movement in 1968. In the West during the 1960s, mostly young students were recruited. This made some sociologists very interested in the movement (John Lofland's research refers to this period). However, proselytism did not enjoy much numerical success.

Nevertheless, it is important to mention that during this period proselytism in the United States differed in style from that in Europe (a study on this was made by Bromley and Shupe) which would cause numerous problems in the 1970s. On the one hand, the "Oakland family" invited potential disciples to spend a weekend at the church during which Unificationism was presented as a message of peace and unity for the world, without much emphasizing the theology and occasionally without mentioning the name of Rev. Moon at all (some would later accuse the church of concealing its true identity). On the other hand, in New

York disciples insisted on teaching the philosophical and theological aspects of the *Divine Principle;* while in Washington, D.C., Unificationists emphasized the movement's political potential as an alternative to Communism. The practical consequences of these differences were fundamental: in California Unificationism seemed vaguely utopian, and this especially attracted students who aspired toward idealism and humanitarianism, while on the East Coast the anti-Communist accent permitted adherents to be in contact with more conservative people.

So the 1970s witnessed marked differences between the group led by Young Oon Kim, which concentrated on theology, and the California group directed by former missionaries to Japan including Sang Ik-Choi. Later, on the East Coast, recruitment techniques which had been used successfully in Japan were adopted: seminars were longer, lasting either a week or a month, after which people were asked to join the movement as full-time members in one of the community centers. The Washington, D.C., group, guided by Colonel Bo Hi Pak, maintained its political anti-Communist stance (in 1969, with this mission in mind, the Freedom Leadership Foundation was founded). A third development in the movement originated with David S. C. Kim, whose primary interest was ecumenism and the unification of all Christian churches.

Rev. Moon traveled to the United States on two occasions, in 1965 and 1969, while on round-the-world tours. The first tour was intended to create "holy grounds"; the second to celebrate mass weddings. In 1971 he started on a new world tour which lasted three years, at the end of which he decided to live in the States. One of the reasons for this move was to settle, if possible, differences among the different styles of the various church branches in the U.S. The

Unification Church interprets these incidents theologically. After twenty years in Korea, which represented the new Israel (i.e., the Old Testament), Rev. Moon and his wife transferred to the U.S., which represented Christianity in its worldwide expansion (i.e., the New Testament).

America became in the years to follow the center of the church's developing activity and of the Unification movement in general. Rev. Moon declared that the reason for his being in America was to remind its citizens about its role as a providential nation for God and the world. For this reason, the themes of his first campaign were "The Day of Hope," "Christianity in Crisis: New Hope," "The New Future of Christianity," and, on the occasion of the bicentennial of the founding of the United States (1976), "God Bless America." The objective of bringing these campaigns to national attention, in spite of certain difficulties, would be fulfilled in the 1970s. The arrival of Rev. Moon in the United States marked, in effect, a decisive development in the Unification movement internally and the expansion of the movement, which at that time had only around 500 American members. At the end of his tour in February 1972, during a meeting in Los Angeles, Rev. Moon personally proposed to his disciples a program of reorganizing the recruitment of members, based on the formation of mobile witnessing teams destined to visit the entire continental United States. This was "The One World Crusade." Also permanent church centers were to be opened in all forty-eight continental states with a national center in the New York area.

The limited success of the 1972 tour pushed the Unification movement to be better organized. According to one of the chief directors, Ken Sudo, who was primarily responsible for gathering a crowd of some 20,000 people in

New York in 1974, 300 Unificationists from the area and 700 from other cities were organized. They worked for two months stopping passers-by on the street and telephoning everyone with whom they had come in contact, putting up posters, distributing flyers, and using many other methods.[8] To put into practice Rev. Moon's new directives, it became necessary to collect large sums of money in a short time. This gave birth to the Mobile Fund-Raising Teams that began going throughout the States and later in other countries, selling flowers, magazines, candles, or simply asking for donations. The funds collected were used to finance the programs and development of the church, and, together with the fruits of industrial and commercial businesses, developed especially in Japan and Korea, were used to buy the Belvedere residence in Tarrytown, New York (a property previously owned by the well-known liquor dynasty, Seagrams). Belvedere was also used as an international training and conference center, and remains to this day the place where Rev. Moon gives Sunday morning services when he is in town. Later the Unification Church bought, again in New York, a property near Barrytown that belonged to the Catholic Brothers of the Christian Schools, and there established a theological seminary. Also from the profits of its different businesses, the Unification Church was able to launch in 1977 the first of its daily newspapers[9]: *The News World*, later renamed *The New York City Tribune* (1976-91). This was followed by the most important daily newspaper with Unificationist connections, *The Washington Times*, founded by Rev. Moon in 1982 after successful test issues in 1981, and a Spanish newspaper in New York, *Noticias del Mundo*.

Rev. Moon's tours of different American cities in 1973, 1974, and 1976 were very visible. Around 300,000 people attended the rally held by the church in the American capital near the Washington Monument on the occasion of the bicentennial of the Declaration of Independence. The theme centered on America's spiritual responsibility to save the world. At the same time, other rallies were taking place in Japan and Korea: on February 8, 1975, Rev. Moon celebrated in Seoul the wedding of 1,800 couples from twenty countries throughout the world. On June 7, again in Seoul, he presided over a rally denouncing North Korea's politics of aggression; some 1 million people attended this event.

In 1973 the church's political ties with American conservatives guided Rev. Moon to support President Richard M. Nixon during the Watergate scandal. Rev. Moon declared that his decision was inspired and was not a political strategy. At different times in 1973 and 1974, thousands of Unificationists fasted and prayed for Nixon. This was not because they considered him innocent, but because they thought that America should forgive its president. Rev. Moon hoped the president would admit his error and that Americans would forgive him and remain united to a conservative leader to halt the advance of Communism as well as moral and social decadence. The motto of the campaign conducted by members of the Unification Church, who demonstrated by fasting and praying for three days in front of the U.S. Capitol, was "Forgive, Love and Unite." On February 1, 1974, Nixon thanked the Unification Church for its support and officially received Sun Myung Moon. The campaign gave the Unification Church its greatest public notoriety, and new anti-Unification press campaigns were launched by Rev. Moon's opponents.

In the United States and other countries, the parents of young followers of the Unification Church, the majority of whom disapproved of their children's choice, organized themselves into associations accusing the Unification Church of "brainwashing." They frequently turned to "de-programmers" who, as noted earlier, arranged for kidnappings followed by "treatments" to convince their children to abandon the church. Controversies, court cases, and further press assaults followed.

In Europe some conservative members of England's parliament began to propose measures against "brainwashing." Tax investigations regarding the Unification Church were conducted in the United States, where some Unificationists were charged in 1978 as a result of the Congressional investigation into the so-called Koreagate scandal. This was an affair relating to the lobbying and corruption of U.S. representatives in favor of the political and economic interests of South Korea. All the Unificationists involved were eventually released without charge. The church's defense hinged on the intervention of Colonel Bo Hi Pak and are described in a book he authored.[10]

Faced with these accusations, which were repeated and amplified in the popular press, the Unification Church energetically defended itself and intensified its propaganda, often in court. In 1981 in London, England, they lost a defamation case against the *Daily Mail*, but in return would subsequently win a certain number of cases in the United States. On February 3, 1988, a four-year investigation by the British government, initiated in response to the verdict in the *Daily Mail* libel case, to remove the charitable status of the two charities comprising the Unification Church in the United Kingdom, was dropped as the evidence was "insufficiently reliable" or of "insufficient weight," according to then-attorney general Sir Patrick Mayhew.[11]

At the same time the Unification Church concentrated

its energies on creating and developing many organizations and foundations. Some of these, created during the last thirty years, are: the International Conference for the Unity of the Sciences (ICUS), the International Cultural Foundation (ICF), and the Professors Academy for World Peace (PWPA). These organizations have promoted international academic conferences, often featuring personalities otherwise unaffiliated with Unificationism. The International Federation for Victory over Communism (IFVOC) and the Freedom Leadership Foundation have promoted international conferences and activities that are anti-Communist in character. The Collegiate Association for the Research of Principles (CARP) undertook student activities. The Assembly of the World's Religions (AWR), the Council for World Religions, and the Youth Seminary on World Religions, later known as the Religious Youth Service, formed part of the church's inter-religious and ecumenical activities, the axis of which was the International Religious Foundation (IRF). These and other organizations have promoted religious and spiritual activities usually of an ecumenical character. In 1991 Rev. Moon reorganized a number of groups into different, new international federations. The Federation for World Peace (FWP) and the Inter-Religious Federation for World Peace (IRFWP) were created more or less simultaneously. The first is responsible for coordinating the activities of Unificationists attached to the political world together with the Summit Council for World Peace. The second promotes inter-religious dialogue through conferences and publications. Among the achievements of IRFWP is the publication of a monumental anthology of sacred scriptures from all the great religions,[12] excerpts which emphasize the common points believed to exist among the religions.

On July 1, 1991, the Unification Church took a new turn with Rev. Moon declaring that now was the beginning of the providence of "Tribal Messiahship." Members already having their own family were encouraged to return to their countries of origin to undertake apostolic work there. Rev. Moon invited "blessed" families (that is, families whose marriages had been celebrated by him), who were already defined as "Tribal Messiahs," to follow teachings taken from Jesus' life and not those from Jacob's life, which had previously been followed. In reality, Rev. Moon asked "blessed" families to pass from a life of service in the wider world to more specific service with their own families and relatives in order to "save" their own "tribes" in their own nations. From a sociological point of view, this change in 1991 confirmed that being a full-time member would now be less crucial.

In December 1991, forty years after Rev. Moon's imprisonment in a forced labor camp, he returned with his wife to North Korea to meet Kim Il Sung, under whose regime he had been tortured and imprisoned. He considered this to be a crucial step for the unification of Korea and for the institution of world peace. Additionally, Unificationists regard the meeting as important because it was the will of Providence and represented the unification of "Cain" and "Abel." In his residence in Hung Nam, the elderly North Korean dictator warmly received the Moons. After forty years, in the same place where he had begun his work in 1951, Rev. Moon declared that in a certain sense he could now conclude his mission by passing it to his wife who, after a few months, would proclaim the beginning of the "era of women's liberation." On the same occasion Rev. Moon returned to the city of his birth and met those of his family who had survived. He was also able to lay flowers on the tomb of his parents, who died under the Communist regime.

Two other organizations were founded between 1992 and 1994: the Women's Federation for World Peace (WFWP) on April 19, 1992, in Seoul, and the Youth Federation for World Peace (YFWP) on July 26, 1994, in Washington, D.C. The first organization under the presidency of Mrs. Hak Ja Han Moon, Rev. Moon's wife, is primarily involved in the struggle against immorality and defending family values by proposing to play an educational role in society, particularly among young people, and promoting the ideal of sexual abstinence before marriage and fidelity after. WFWP, which promotes charitable, humanitarian activities and racial and international peace events, was granted Category 1 NGO consultative status by the Economic and Social Department of the United Nations in 1997. With regard to charity, the International Relief Friendship Foundation (IRFF) is also acknowledged as a nongovernmental organization by the United Nations and has helped Cambodian refugees as well as different populations in Latin America in emergency situations following natural disasters. Other foundations are active in the artistic field. Among musical groups are the Go World Brass Band, the Korean Folk Ballet, the New Hope Singers International, the New York Symphony Orchestra, and especially the children's ballet, the Little Angels, a creation of the church's Korean Culture and Freedom Foundation, later associated with a primary school bearing the same name. This school, although inspired by Unification principles, is not directly connected with the church, and a majority of students are from non-Unificationist families. The Little Angels ballet has performed at UNICEF, the White House, the Vatican, and the London Palladium for Queen Elizabeth II. The most prestigious artistic institution of the

Unification movement is the Universal Ballet Company. The academy, established in Washington, D.C., teaches classic Russian ballet, thanks to maestro choreographer Oleg Vinogradov.

In the 1980s, the Confederation of the Associations for the Unification of the Americas, or CAUSA, extended its activity to the entire world, developing different cultural and political projects with an anti-Communist orientation. At the beginning of the 1950s, the International Federation for Victory over Communism (IFVOC) was founded in Korea. In 1976, at the end of the American bicentennial campaign, Rev. Moon concluded with a promise to members that one day he would organize "a great rally for God in the Soviet Capital." In 1980 CAUSA was founded in America, and in August 1985 in Geneva, almost 200 people, academics and experts, met to debate the theme "The situation in the world after the fall of the communist empire." This meeting was organized by the Professors World Peace Academy. In August 1987 the student association, CARP, led 3,000 young demonstrators in Berlin, who asked Communist leaders to bring down the Berlin Wall. In April 1990, at a conference organized by the World Media Association, AULA, and the Summit Council for World Peace, leaders and journalists from all over the world met to discuss freedom of the press in Moscow, where the politics of *glasnost* and *perestroika* had already begun. On April 16, 1990, during an official meeting with President Gorbachev, the Reverend and Mrs. Moon embraced Gorbachev in front of photographers. This meeting was perceived by Rev. Moon as having theological importance and represented an historic meeting on a worldwide level between Esau and Jacob. After the dismantlement of the Soviet Empire, the activities of CAUSA have diminished substantially, and the association is no longer a priority of Unificationists. They are now more centered on the fight against sexual permissiveness, which they consider to be the ultimate battle between God and the forces of evil. CAUSA was born from Unificationism and was sustained by the church with people and means, but also among its directors were many non-Unificationists. It was in this capacity, for example, that two ambassadors, both Roman Catholics, were among CAUSA's greatest activists.

One cannot reasonably affirm that this confederation had proselytism as its objective; on the other hand, it seems improbable that among the conservative political and cultural personalities involved in CAUSA were men and women who would not consider changing their religion. Still, very little if any proselyting on behalf of the Unification Church was ever accomplished by CAUSA.

Similar considerations may be attached to the Association for the Unity of Latin America (AULA), inaugurated and organized by members of the Unification Church. However, AULA is composed of numerous prestigious political Latin-American personalities, many of whom are often far removed from the history and mentality of Unificationism. Participants at an international congress of AULA were received in a special audience by Pope John Paul II at the Vatican on December 6, 1985. Evidently, no one thought this audience implied that the Holy See supported the Unification Church.

There are also commercial activities belonging to the Unification Church in which Unificationists work but are in the minority. Before going bankrupt in the 1998 Far East financial crisis, the best known of such activities were the machine industry Tong Il in Korea and the society for producing dietary supplements Il Wha, the largest world distributor of Korean ginseng. At Tong Il weapons parts were made, causing considerable controversy. The church responded that these activities were a means of patriotic collaboration with the national defense of a country still technically at war with North Korea. This, the church said, was normal in South Korea for all businesses. In the United States, the church has developed different activities in the areas of marine work and fishing. According to newspaper reports from Korea, on August 31, 1999, Hong Kong-based and Unification-affiliated Pyonghwa Motors received initial permission to develop plans to invest $300 million to build cars in North Korea. Pyonghwa hopes first to establish a car repair facility in the North.

But controversies continued. As has been the case with other religious movements, it was the U.S. Internal Revenue Service—on the insistence of an influential Republican from Kansas, Bob Dole, who twenty years later would become a U.S. presidential candidate—that responded to charges from anti-cult movements. In 1976 the American fiscal administration centered its attention on the personal bank account of Sun Myung Moon, which was made up of funds donated by his disciples. An examination concluded that Rev. Moon had paid tax on only a portion of the interest generated by his account. Denying that the interest referred to a sum which belonged to a religious organization, and in this case would be exempted from federal tax, the IRS argued that this was the personal fund of Rev. Moon, who therefore was guilty of tax fraud (estimated at $7,300). This sum could hardly be regarded as significant when one realizes that the financial statement of the Unification Church in America was in the millions of dollars. That sum was nevertheless sufficient, using a strict application of American tax law, to bring Rev. Moon to trial and to proceed to his conviction and imprisonment.

In the first instance, the district attorney was able to have Rev. Moon judged by a jury and not by a court composed of judges. This request gave rise to a series of controversies because Rev. Moon's defense lawyers maintained that it would be difficult, if not impossible, to find people free from prejudice regarding such a controversial figure. In spite of all the protests—and the belief of three separate commissions of experts—Rev. Moon was found guilty of tax fraud and condemned to eighteen months' imprisonment. In 1982 two of the three judges comprising the federal Court of Appeals upheld the sentence. On May 13, 1984, the U.S. Supreme Court refused to review the case. On June 20, 1984, Rev. Moon entered the penitentiary in Danbury, Connecticut. His imprisonment was reduced by five months for good conduct and he left on August 20, 1985. On the same day the president of the Moral Majority, the Reverend Jerry Falwell, and the Reverend Joseph Lowery, president of the Southern Christian Leadership Conference, held a press conference in support of Rev. Moon. That evening Rev. Moon's release was celebrated during a banquet in Washington, D.C., attended by 1,700 religious figures from different denominations and faiths.

The presence at the same table of Falwell and Lowery, two of the most celebrated representatives of the "conservative" and "liberal" wings of American Protestantism, at a press conference in favor of the leader of Unificationism demonstrated that something had changed in the attitude of religious circles towards Rev. Moon. In the meantime in Italy, Ilario Martella, a district attorney with the Court of Rome (noted for having investigated the attempt on the Pope's life), after a full report by the police which was prompted by claims made by the parents of young Unificationists, who accused the church of fraud and "brainwashing," declared that there was insufficient evidence for the investigation to continue, that the allegations were groundless.

Paradoxically, the case against Rev. Moon for tax fraud had, in a decisive way, contributed to positive change in American public opinion towards the Unification Church. In fact, the violations of religious liberties in the case of Rev. Moon were so evident that the *New York Times*, previously a vocal critic of Unificationism and its political stance, wrote on May 20, 1984, that the sentencing of Rev. Moon signalled the triumph of "legal theories that offer tempting opportunities for interference in church affairs under the banner of criminal tax prosecution."[13] The most anti-Unificationist paper in the United States, the *Washington Post*, also reported the opinion prevailing among watchdog organizations in areas of religious liberty and human rights that "Moon's conviction represents a threat to all religious groups, but especially to those whose clergy are poor and unsophisticated and whose theology is unorthodox."[14]

Controversies of a political nature have also lost since then some of their intensity. Some of the journalists who were prepared to conduct campaigns against the Unification Church were motivated by liberal political attitudes and were hostile to the church's staunch anti-Communism. After 1989, for obvious reasons, anti-Communism was no longer at the center of Unificationists' interests. Even this modification was explained theologically in a talk which Unificationists considered to be crucial and which was disseminated throughout the world. That same discourse was read by Mrs. Moon to members of the U.S. Congress in Washington, D.C., on July 28, 1993, to representatives of the General Assembly of the United Nations on September 7, 1993, and to parliamentary and political leaders of different nations, including South Korea, Canada, Brazil, and India. After the Moons' meetings with Communist leaders Kim Il Sung and Gorbachev—which, we have seen, for Unificationists had a significance beyond politics—the Unification Church claimed that the East-West conflict was the result of what happened at the beginning of recorded history between Cain and Abel. This can be resolved not only on the Korean national level, but also on the worldwide level. The "providence of restoration," as Rev. Moon calls it, can now change its focus to solving an even older conflict, that of Adam and Eve. From there, a change of priority can now take place—moving away from Communism and toward the problems of immorality. Naturally, these complex interpretations, where international politics can be traced to both biblical characters and Rev. Moon, are comprehensible only if one remembers that, for Unificationists, their leader is not just a simple religious teacher but the Lord of the Second Advent.

Today the fight for family values and against pornography occupies the Unificationist agenda. This may make it easier to dialogue with certain Evangelical groups, even if they are far removed from the Unification Church's theology. In France the end of the anti-Communist mission as a priority of the church led to a severing of ties with the right-wing National Front, ties which at one time were quite visible. These ties, which had permitted a Unificationist personality, Pierre Ceyrac, to be elected as a deputy for northern France, and then as a member of the European Parliament, had created international controversy.[15]

The fact that Unificationism is today a movement less active on the political stage, and with few members employed full time by the church, brings the movement closer to the structural features of many other religious organizations. However, Unificationism maintains a universalistic attitude and tries to present itself as the center of a worldwide movement for morality, particularly sexual morality. It is above all the Women's Federation for World Peace that has increased the movement's activities in this field, particularly with the collaboration of former U.S. president George Bush and his wife, Barbara, who in 1994 accompanied Mrs. Moon on a tour of Japan. Obviously many Evangelical organizations opposed to "cults" have actively protested the participation of a "cult" such as the Unification Church in interdenominational activities promoting chastity (Evangelical organizations assemble millions of young Americans based on the slogan "Let love wait").

In the spring of 1994, two meetings took place in Seoul. In March the Federation for World Peace organized the second conference on world peace, and a delegation of participants visited North Korean leader Kim Il-Sung a few days before his death. The other meeting, on April 28-30, was organized by the Inter-Religious Federation for World Peace around the theme "Evil in the different religious visions."

The mid-1990s was a time of significant change for the Unification movement. They first saw the Reverend and Mrs. Moon shift the focus of their activity from North America to South America. In numerous speeches Rev. Moon referred to North America as the Protestant North Europe and Latin America as the Catholic Southern Europe. Rev. Moon claims to support the "greater unification" of the Americas before attention can shift towards Europe and Africa. There has been greater missionary activity in Latin America and considerable financial investment in Uruguay. This has alarmed the Catholic church in some countries. There have been campaigns in the Latin

American media, for example, to ban foreign Unificationist missionaries.

One the most significant Unificationist projects in South America is the New Hope Farm Project, now called New Hope East Garden. Referred to locally as paradise on earth, the region of the Miranda and Plata rivers captured the imagination of the Reverend and Mrs. Moon, when they were fishing in the untamed forest of western Brazil, as a "Garden of Eden." At the center of the South American continent, one area is indeed an untouched paradise, while another is deforested and polluted. The New Hope East Garden Project aims to provide both moral and formal education for residents and visitors, culminating in long-distance learning projects operated in cooperation with the University of Bridgeport in the United States.[16]

The New Hope East Garden hopes to diversify land use from ranching to a variety of crops in thirty-three areas around the region. The development of fish farms, the reclamation of flora and fauna, reforestation, and a wider mix of crops accompanied by agricultural research and skills education are seen as the means to revitalize the misuse of this fertile land. Having invested $25 million and bought 7.5 million acres of land, according to Cesar Zeduski, spokesman for the project, the New Hope East Garden is developing across the state with the rapid construction of buildings.

Dr. Tyler Hendricks, the U.S. president of the Family Federation for World Peace and Unification (FFWPU), wrote that "Rev. Sun Myung Moon views the New Hope East Garden as the zero (i.e., beginning) point for the Kingdom of Heaven on Earth. There are millions of empty square miles between São Paolo, Buenos Aires, and Campo Grande. They are verdant, luxuriant plains and hills and valleys. They await the loving and strong hand of a true owner, who can make them abundant for the sake of a hungry world."[17]

It is unclear to what extent members may be called to immigrate to Mato Grosso do Sul. "Blessed families" have been asked to attend a forty-day workshop at the New Hope East Garden and have their photographs taken with the Reverend and Mrs. Moon as one qualification for "registration for Heaven." Two conferences on "Preservation and Sustainable Development in the Pantanal" were organized in 1999 and a Website was opened on this subject (www.pantanal.org).

The second development has been the repentance movement at Chung Pyung Workshop Centre in South Korea. Chung Pyung had long been a holy ground, but since 1995 workshops there began to liberate Unificationists from evil spirits. Mrs. Moon's deceased mother, called Dae Mo Nim (Great Mother) by Unificationists, is said to cooperate from the spiritual world with a medium, Mrs. Hyo Nam Kim, who leads the workshops. With the assistance of angels, many spirits are said to be encouraged to leave Unificationists' bodies and go to the spiritual world for a *Divine Principle* workshop led by Heung Jin Moon, the Reverend and Mrs. Moon's son who died in a car crash in 1984. By the beginning of 1999, over 300 three-day workshops and thirty forty-day workshops had taken place and more than 250,000 members had participated. There are a number of testimonies of miraculous physical healings as well as people claiming to have seen angels or the liberation of resentful spirits from their bodies.[18]

A further recent development has been the claim of liberation, education, and blessing of ancestors, which has become a regular feature of both the Chung Pyung seminars and Mrs. Hyo Nam Kim's visits to other nations. Until September 1999, liberation ceremonies were exclusively directed at the first seven generations of members' ancestors on the father's side, with subsequent plans for further ceremonies to liberate up to 120 generations. There are indications that liberation ceremonies for ancestors on the mother's side will soon be available. For blessed members who have had children who died, there is an occasional ceremony to connect to their children in the spirit world, where they can grow and mature up to a point where they can then be matched with a partner and blessed.

The Chung Pyung Workshop Centre is also where a Unificationist temple has been built holding 10,000 people. This was completed in preparation for Rev. Moon's 80th birthday, solemnly celebrated on February 10, 2000. It is seen by Unificationists as providentially significant in relation to King Solomon's temple. The fact that it was built by the voluntary donations of those participating in the workshops at Chung Pyung is also seen as significant.

Through the Chung Pyung Workshops, a new type of "blessing" has been initiated. The "Heaven and Earth Blessing" is said to allow the spirit of a spouse who has died to return to live with the widower who remains on the earth. According to speeches by Rev. Chung Hwan Kwak and Mrs. Hyo Nam Kim, the liberation of resentful spirits has been followed by their education and then "blessing" in the spiritual world. Billions of spirits are said to have been "blessed."

The spirit world seems paramount among Rev. Moon's most recent concerns. The messages of San Hung Lee from the spirit world are, in this respect, "integral to a providential event. The fifth chapter [of the book containing Lee's messages] is a record of Lee's interviews, at Rev. Moon's request, with mostly infamous personages—Lenin, Stalin, Hitler, etc. Within a month of that communication, at the blessing of 120 million couples on June 30, 1998, these same personages were blessed as the representatives of all wicked people, thereby opening the gate for the 'liberation of Hell.'"[19]

Beginning in 1995, Rev. Moon brought many senior Korean leaders of the Unification Church to forty-day workshops at Chung Pyung. At the conclusion, Rev. Moon initiated what he called National Messiahship. Each nation is to be led by a group of four families: one from Korea, one from Japan, one from America or Great Britain or France, and one from Germany or Austria or Italy. Elder couples, who volunteered to participate after attending the workshop in Chung Pyung, chose their country by lottery. They were told to live in that country from that time on and to encourage their descendants also to live there to restore it for God. This has become a major change in the structure of the Unification movement.

On May 1, 1994, the fortieth anniversary of the foundation of the Holy Spirit Association for the Unification of World Christianity was celebrated in Seoul. According to Rev. Moon, this event represented the attainment of a fundamental stage in his movement's history, which permitted him to declare the conclusion of the "cycle" of the Unification Church as the pre-eminent body of the Unification movement. He then inaugurated the Family Federation for World Peace and Unification which combines all the organizations Rev. Moon has created. Rev. Moon affirms that the "course" of religion is finished and that, with the beginning of the new era of the family, God will now meet humankind in the family. At this time it was also declared that people should campaign for the purification of love and the sanctification of the family. Thus other religious organizations which possess similar ethical standards will be invited to participate in this umbrella organization. The Unification Church will continue, in order to support the religious functions of its members, as the Unification Family Church— one of the many religious organizations within the FFWPU. With these changes, one may wonder what the implications are for the future of the Unification Church as a religious organization.

The year 1998 also saw less pleasant developments for the Unification movement. As a result of the Asian economic crisis, but also of internal mismanagement, a number of businesses of the Tong Il group in Korea collapsed under the weight of massive debts. Nansook Hong, the divorced wife of Reverend and Mrs. Moon's elder son Hyo Jin Moon, penned a book, *In the Shadow of the Moons*,[20] ghost-written by Eileen McNamara, a journalist from the *Boston Globe* who had published a number of critical stories about Unificationism. The book depicts Nansook's fourteen years of marriage to Hyo Jin as plagued by her husband's drug use, adultery, and in the end physical violence. Although at the end of bitter divorce proceedings, one cannot expect either party to be truly objective, Hong's tale of abuse is credible, and the Unification Church acknowledged Hyo Jin's personal problems well before publication of the book (Hyo Jin was "reblessed" to a new wife, Yun Ah Choi, on February 5, 1999, in Seoul, the first instance of "reblessing" among the "True Children" of the Reverend and Mrs. Moon).

More serious was Hong's charge that, while promoting family values in their teachings, the Reverend and Mrs. Moon lost control of their own family, as evidenced by Hyo Jin's addiction problems and by the fact that other "True Children" left or became inactive in the church. (Sadly, another "True Child" died falling out a hotel window in Reno, Nevada, later in 1999; the family termed it an "incident," the media a suicide.) The Reverend and Mrs. Moon have admitted responsibility for the problems of some of their children, stating that the task of their worldwide ministry demanded the sacrifice of their family. Nansook's book offers a bitter portrait of Mrs. Moon and accuses Rev. Moon of sexual misconduct during his life, including fathering an illegitimate child. The Unification Church answered that Rev. Moon "never violated the Principle nor violated his responsibility as the messianic protector of True Love," noting also that "Father [i.e., Rev. Moon] has taught extensively about the complicated biblical and providential history of the restoration of blood lineage, including the role of such providential figures as Jacob (Rachel and Leah and servants), Tamar (and her father-in-law, Judah) and others in fulfilling conditions in this area."[21] Other figures such as Abraham (Sarah and Hagar) and King David (Bethsheba) have also been mentioned. This "complicated history" includes Rev. Moon and his family, whose life—the church implies—cannot be judged by ordinary human standards. This, the church insists, does not in any way give permission to members to violate their blessing and the *Divine Principle*'s fundamental standard of one man and one woman for eternity. Regardless, a number of members have been deeply disturbed by Hong's book.

The issue of succession is of fundamental importance. Rev. Moon turned eighty years old in 2000 (or, by Korean age calculations, in 1999). Mrs. Moon is fifty-seven years old. Since 1992 she has taken a more visible role, particularly in three world speaking tours in 1992, 1993, and 1999. Mrs. Moon has also spoken on Capitol Hill, at the United Nations, and in other parliaments around the world. Her relative youth and the respect with which she is held by the membership will be a point of stability for the Unification movement. The ceremony to inaugurate the Reverend and Mrs. Moon's third son, Hyun Jin Moon, as vice president of the Family Federation for World Peace and Unification International on July 19, 1998, as well as his responsibility to educate the "second generation," denotes him as the successor. Hyun Jin Moon had represented the Republic of Korea in the Olympic equestrian event in 1988 and 1992. He graduated from the Harvard Business School with an M.B.A. in 1998. Rev. Moon joked during his address that he is criticized for having "failed in business ventures, but now I have a son who with an M.B.A. who will be successful in business." Hyun Jin Moon's blessing to the daughter of Rev. Chung Hwan Kwak (Rev. Moon's assistant and former president of the FFWPUI), Jun Sook Kwak, is also a significant point of continuity.

A new organization was inaugurated on February 6, 1999, in Seoul. The Inter-religious and International Federation for World Peace's mission is "to implement a system through which the highest expressions of religious wisdom are brought to the table at which the world's most serious and urgent problems are being addressed ... by creating a council of religious leaders within the framework of the United Nations."[22] Rev. Moon sees the IIFWP as a body which will campaign to recreate the United Nations as a truly bicameral institution. Since 1999 the IIFWP has sponsored the Hoon Dok Hae (Gathering for Reading and Learning) conferences for academics, religious leaders, and politicians devoted to reconsidering Reverend Moon's thought and career. On June 15, 1999, Reverend Sun Jo Hwang became the new president of FFWPUI, replacing Reverend Kwak who became the president of the IIFWP. Reverend

Sun Jo Hwang, who was a professor of theology at Unificationist Sun Moon University, is a relatively young leader who participated in the Blessing of 1982. He believes in the Internet as a missionary tool and has promoted a new Website based in Korea: the Completed Testament News at http://family.tongil.or.kr/ctnews. He has also promoted the use of live Internet audio or video transmissions to show important ceremonies.

Also in 1999, three important "Declarations" were released, all illustrating the increasing importance of numerology and dispensationalism in Reverend Moon's thinking. A "Jeol" is a Holy Day Commemoration in the Unification Movement. Reverend and Mrs. Moon gave a special benediction at nine minutes and nine seconds past 9:00 a.m. on September 9, 1999. Moon's age being seventy-nine, the number nine appeared nine times, and the day was celebrated as "9.9 Jeol." The number nine previously "belonged" to Satan and was an evil number, but the 9.9 Jeol ceremonies rescued it for God, allowing also the liberation of many souls in the spirit world. 9.9 Jeol was regarded as a connecting point between the "Declaration Day of the Realm of Cosmic Sabbath for Parents of Heaven and Earth" on 7.8 Jeol and the "Proclamation of the Celebration of Cosmic Victory." 7.8 Jeol had earlier been celebrated at seven minutes and seven seconds past 7:00 a.m. on July 7, 1997, and inaugurated events capable of recreating the original world under God's sovereignty. Reverend Moon proclaimed 3.10 Jeol at ten minutes past 10:00 a.m. on September 10, 1999. With 3.10 Jeol, all numbers from one to ten were finally restored as Heaven's numbers. This marked an event of great eschatological significance, since God can now restore "the original world of creation by numbers." The new leader of the Unification movement,

Reverend Sun Jo Hwang, seems to concentrate his message, after the problems and controversies of 1998, on the cosmic significance of the dates of 7.8 Jeol, 9.9 Jeol, and 3.10 Jeol. Other teachings emphasized by Rev. Moon in the last few years deal with the sacred nature of sexuality in general and the sexual organs in particular. Although these teachings correspond to centuries-old Korean traditions, they became easy targets for Evangelical counter-cultists.

Rev. Sun Myung Moon's middle school portrait
(ca. early 1930s).

Rev. Moon cooks for fellow lodgers. From left to right are Yoo Koo-bok; Moon's cousin Seung-gyun; Kwon Duk-pal (standing), the preacher at the church Moon attended; and Moon.

The shack Rev. Moon built with ration boxes in Pusan in 1951.

Rev. Moon with early followers, including an American G.I., in the 1950s.

Rev. Moon with early followers in Pusan. From left to right are Ok Se-hyun; Moon; Chi Seung-do; and Kim Won-pil (seated).

Rev. Moon teaching his followers in Korea in the late 1950s.

Old Korean church headquarters in Seoul.

Rev. Moon, his wife, and followers outside the old Seoul church.

Rev. Moon in prayer in the early 1960s.

The first fishing boat.

Rev. Moon and Hak Ja Han on their wedding day, April 11, 1960.

The Welcome Home ceremony from Rev. Moon's first world tour.

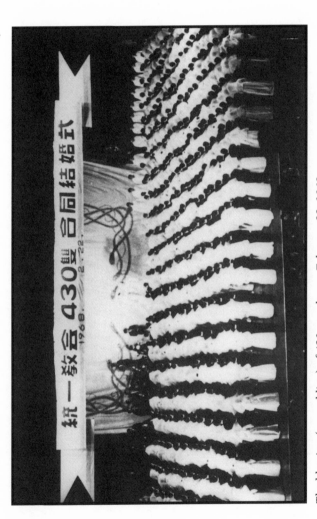

The blessing (or wedding) of 430 couples on February 22, 1968.

Rev. Moon arrives in America for one of his tours in the early 1970s.

An anti-communist rally on Yoida Island.

Rev. Moon waves to followers at the Yankee Stadium rally in 1976 (following is Bo Hi Pak).

The blessing (or wedding) of 2,075 couples in Madison Square Garden in 1982.

Rev. and Mrs. Moon meet Mikail Gorbachev in the Kremlin in 1990.

3.

Doctrine

In the Unification Church, Sunday morning worship nor-mally consists of Bible reading. This is followed by read-ing the *Divine Principle*. According to the *Divine Principle*: "Scriptures, however, are not the truth itself but textbooks teaching the truth."[1]

> The New Testament is but an interim textbook given to en-lighten the people of two thousand years ago, whose spiri-tual and intellectual levels were far lower than today. The modern, scientific-minded thirst for the truth cannot be couched in symbols and parables aimed specifically at in-structing the people of an earlier age. For the modern, intel-lectual people to be enlightened in the truth, there must ap-pear another textbook of higher and richer content, with a more scientific method of expression.[2]

In the modern world, the Bible is no longer sufficient—not because it does not teach the truth, but because its lan-guage is obscure and risks giving way to different and in-conceivable interpretations. It is for this that "a new ex-pression of truth must appear" to "shed new light" on what the Bible expressed only partly. This new expression of "truth should be able to unify knowledge by reconciling the internal truth pursued by religion and the external truth pursued by science."[3] The *Divine Principle* is made up precisely of this new expression of truth. From the time the *Divine Principle* appeared, Christians have been urged to accept it and not to remain tied to the Bible as the only expression of truth. Christians today should behave in the same way as the disciples of Jesus: "there was not one who was overly attached to the Old Testament Scriptures."[4]

On the other hand, the *Divine Principle* claims as its mission the unification not only of the different branches of Christianity (which occupies a central responsibility in God's providence), but also of all other religions. As early as 1980, for example, a volume of the *Principle* was published from an Islamic perspective, in which biblical quotations are less numerous. There is even a chapter on the special role of Islam, while the amount of space devoted to Jesus Christ is reduced.[5]

The fundamental question which all men and women must answer to understand the universe is that regarding the nature of God. God is invisible, but may be observed from the visible nature of his creation. According to the *Divine Principle,* the fundamental nature of the creation is its duality—between "subject" and "object" (the *Divine Principle* defines "subject" as the pole which begins a relation, "object" as the pole which responds to the subject's initiative), masculine and feminine, positive and negative, the internal nature (*sung sang* in Korean) and external form (*hyung sang* in Korean) of every human being. From this dual aspect of creation, the *Divine Principle* concludes that duality is a fundamental attribute of God. God has within himself interior and exterior, positive and negative, masculine and feminine, love and beauty. The dual aspects of God are revealed in the creation of the world, whose structure is fundamentally dualistic. This duality also manifests itself in every being which possesses at the same time an internal character and external form. The reciprocal relationship between creatures depends fundamentally on the action of "give and take" which originates from the "Universal Prime Force" beginning in God and culminates in a reciprocal relationship of "subject" and "object" in everything that exists on the earth.

Humans, more than any other creature, are created to be God's object of love, the most important aspect of his divinity. Therefore, to permit men and women to become truly the object of God's love, God gave them three blessings: the capacity to perfect their character, the possibility to realize an ideal family and society centered on God, and the right to have dominion over the creation (this is how the *Divine Principle* interprets the words God gave to Adam and Eve in Genesis 1:28: "Be fruitful and multiply and fill the earth and subdue it"). Without sin the first parents would have fulfilled these three responsibilities and established the Kingdom of God on earth, thus fully realizing God's ideal.

Original sin, according to Unificationist doctrine, stems from the "four position foundation," which is the principle or fundamental structure through which God works. It deals with the relationship which unites God as subject, as object, and as new creation, which is the result of the union of subject and object. According to the divine plan, the first parents should not have united sexually until they had first completed the process of growth and understanding and received God's "blessing" (permission). Only on that basis would their union have constituted a "four position foundation" centered on God. But because of their premature union, Adam and Eve formed a "four position foundation" centered on the fallen angel Lucifer or Satan, who by seducing Eve initiated the process of the Fall. This provoked grave consequences for all humankind because the fruit of their union, from which we result, belongs to the blood lineage of the fallen angel.

But the Fall did not mean that God would abandon his original plan. On the contrary, he works to reconstruct the true "four position foundation." After the Fall the will of God was to restore humanity to its unfallen state. Therefore the history of humankind became the history of the "providence of salvation"—that is, of God's attempt—often hindered by a lack of cooperation from women and men—to accomplish the "last days," the period in which humanity could fulfil the original three blessings.

Throughout history, the opportunity to make an offering has been presented to representative individuals, families, nations, or, in some cases, religions or even a whole gender (male or female) at predetermined intervals. These are the occasions to fulfill the foundation necessary to receive the Messiah, who completes the mission that Adam failed to fulfill. The *Divine Principle* explains that the course of history is modelled on various events which must direct history towards the coming of the Messiah and the realization of the Kingdom of God in heaven and on earth. However, when a chosen individual, family, or nation fails, even if only partly, to realize the mission, the providential period is prolonged and God calls a successor to complete that mission. A new providential period thus begins. This new providential figure must follow a similar course to the one who failed, though the person and place are not the same. In the system of the *Divine Principle,* history is predetermined in its mission but the historical intervals and personalities are not fixed. The intervals are either completed or prolonged according to the success or failure of the person, family, or nation called to realize a specific mission. These occasions were offered to the family of Adam, the family of Noah, to Abraham, and to Moses. These people, although they made substantial contributions, did not fulfill all the conditions that God requested, thereby losing the heavenly opportunities to receive the Messiah on earth. This made it necessary, therefore, to prolong the history of "restoration" as the chosen individuals, families, or nations did not complete their missions or remedy their partial failures.

Finally, the great Hebrew prophet Elijah appeared to support John the Baptist to help prepare the way of the Lord. However, as further clarified by Rev. Moon in speeches given in 1996-97, John's mission was complicated by the relationship of Mary, Elizabeth, and Zechariah.[6] Unificationists believe that Zechariah fathered both John the Baptist and Jesus. Elizabeth at first accepted Heaven's will to allow her cousin Mary to have sex with her husband, Zechariah, but later could not accept the difficult role Heaven expected of her by maintaining her love for Mary. Mary, pregnant and unmarried, had to leave the protection of the temple. Later, due to the breakdown of relationships between the two families, it was not possible for Jesus to marry John the Baptist's younger sister,[7] as had been God's will, and John had difficulty appreciating Jesus given his own family background. (The *Divine Principle*, on the other hand, implies that John's views on the Law and his asceticism were just as if not more problematic in his ability to accept Jesus' more open-minded teachings.)

Ultimately John the Baptist failed in his mission—he did not understand his role as an Elijah and doubted the qualification of Jesus as the Messiah. Deprived of the preparatory mission of John the Baptist, the Messiah Jesus Christ began his mission in an unfavorable position and for this reason had to face many trials and tribulations. In the end, Israel did not accept Jesus but, on the contrary, instigated his condemnation and death. Therefore, world restoration through the Messiah was not completely realized. Nevertheless, according to Unificationism, the mission of Jesus must not be considered a loss. From the temporal point of view, in order to free humans from the slavery of original sin transmitted at birth, the second advent of the Messiah was necessary. From a spiritual point of view, Jesus perfectly completed his mission because of his total obedience to God. After his resurrection, which completed the spiritual function of Messiah, Jesus became the spiritual "True Father" of believers, while at Pentecost the Holy Spirit occupied the position of a spiritual "True Mother." Those who follow the spiritual "True Parents"—Jesus and the Holy Spirit—obtain spiritual salvation. However, the physical world and the physical body of the believers "can still be invaded by evil," because "original sin still exists in man." This is why the Messiah must return to earth through the "Lord of the Second Advent" to bring to humans a complete salvation, both spiritual and physical, beyond the fundamental but limited salvation that was possible through Jesus.

The christological doctrine of the Unification Church is derived from what has been said before.

> Jesus may well be called God because, as a man who has realized the purpose of creation and who lives in oneness with God, he has a divine nature. Nevertheless, he is not God Himself. The relationship between God and Jesus may be thought of as analogous to the relationship between the mind and the body. Because the body is the substantial object partner to the mind, resembles the mind and acts in

oneness with the mind, it may be understood to be the mind's second self; but it is not the mind itself. By analogy, since Jesus is one with God and the incarnation of God, he may be understood to be God's second self; but he is not God.[8]

Regarding the earthly mission of Jesus, it was not his original purpose to die on the cross but was a secondary course when all possibility of fulfilling the original will was tragically exhausted. The crucifixion of Jesus was the consequence of the blindness of the Jewish leadership and the failure of John the Baptist.[9]

The Lord of the Second Advent will make possible both spiritual and physical salvation. On the basis of a series of numerological considerations and historical parallels between world history after Jesus Christ and the biblical history of Israel, the *Divine Principle* affirms that the period of preparation for the Second Advent must last about 400 years, which began in 1517, the year of the beginning of the Protestant Reformation. The Lord of the Second Advent must be a man born on earth; his essential mission is to establish a perfect family on earth. Once grafted to this family, human beings will finally have children born free of original sin.

The *Divine Principle* concludes, without revealing his identity, that the Lord of the Second Advent was probably born between 1917 and 1930 in Korea. Nevertheless, in Unification literature, beginning in 1960, Rev. Moon and his wife Hak Ja Han, whom he married on April 11, 1960, are often referred to as the "True Parents." In the same way, Unification wedding ceremonies celebrated by Rev. Moon and his wife affirm that the couples are grafted to the matrimony of the "True Parents," thus becoming "blessed families." Before

1992 literature available to the public on Unificationism generally did not openly present Rev. Moon as the Messiah, although undoubtedly the majority of Unificationists considered him as such. From 1992 (and also before in a less systematic and explicit way), Rev. Moon and his wife declared, in their public talks, that together they had completed the mission of the "True Parents" of humankind. The first public declaration in which the "True Parents" outlined their messianic role was made at the World Cultural and Sports Festival (WCSF) in Seoul in 1992. This affirmation was presented worldwide in January 1993 during a series of conferences. The Moons published a discourse entitled "The True Parents and the Completed Testament Era." The Unification Church views January 1993 as beginning the first year of the New Era of the Completed Testament.

4.

Spirituality and Missionary Activities

Recruitment practices and missions of the Unification Church have been the object of important sociological studies by David G. Bromley and Anson D. Shupe (in the United States) and Eileen Barker (in England). They have carried out studies "from inside," living for a few days or months in different Unificationist centers. Their studies show differences between the missionary style of the "Oakland Family," which operated near San Francisco in the 1970s and represented a particular current in the Unification Church, and the methods employed in other parts of the world during different periods. The studies of Bromley and Shupe concluded that accusations against the church regarding these differences derived in great part from techniques used during a certain period by the "Oakland Family," where some missionaries did not speak of Rev. Moon in their first contacts with young people interested in the message. These missionaries more or less concentrated on human values in general. Beginning in 1980, according to instructions from the church, all those invited to a seminar anywhere in the world must now be informed directly that they are studying the teachings of Rev. Moon. Also the so-called technique of "love bombing," once vividly criticized and which, according to Bromley and Shupe, consisted of "showering the person with kindness, special attention, great courtesy and expressions of love,"[1] was mostly practiced in California.

Nevertheless, statistics confirm that the Unification Church did not have in its possession irresistible recruiting techniques. In the cases studied by Eileen Barker, only 10 percent of those who accepted to go to a church center went ahead and participated in a seminar;[2] out of every 100 participants at a two-day seminar, only about thirty or so participated in seven-day seminars; eighteen continued on to twenty-one day courses; while only ten eventually became full-time members. The Unification Church's missionary results are not bad compared to other religious organizations. But it would be an error to describe their techniques as "irresistible" (so "irresistible" that only the hypothesis of "brainwashing" can explain them) or even as very effective, when 90 percent of people exposed to the church in fact resist joining.

Until the mid-1980s, in the West and in Japan (the situation has always been different in Korea) the majority of Unification Church membership consisted of full-time members. This situation later changed in a very visible way, particularly because members were older and family responsibilities forced many to seek jobs. Today in Europe and the United States, many members have regular jobs. Among younger people who belong to the church, those who are students are today generally encouraged to continue their studies. Only a few who have national responsibilities, like "pastors" or those with specific local responsibilities, are still full-time members and are supported financially by the tithes paid by other members.

The presence of full-time and part-time members side-by-side, and the mobility of members who frequently change responsibility and centers, may help explain the difficulty of calculating the precise number of members and the disparity between the number of 3 million adherents so often quoted by Unificationists and the figures mentioned by some scholars of less than 250,000 members throughout the world, mostly in Korea and Japan.

This disparity may also be explained due to the recent evolution of the Unification Church, which renders studies dating from the 1970s and 1980s obsolete. Young people of the 1970s are now around forty and fifty years old. Both in the United States and in Asia, the Unification movement has transformed itself into a more mature movement, one more closely reflecting the classic religious community, where full-time members (priests, pastors, and others) do not comprise the majority in relationship to the simple "faithful" who spend their time working outside the church. Besides—and this makes certain studies in the past even more obsolete—in countries where Unificationism is stronger (Korea and Japan), it does not seem to have as its main objective the proselyting of young people, but rather the giving of support to cultural initiatives which began in the Unification Church and are conducted in cooperation with people of other religious faiths.

Compared to the rituals and practices of other religious movements, those of the Unification Church are often relatively simple. The most important are the public marriages during which the couples, already married in other rites or chosen by Rev. Moon (men and women may refuse that choice and attend another matching ceremony) share a cup of "consecrated wine" in symbolism of their eternal and indissolvable union. These weddings are officiated by Rev. Moon and his wife. On July 1, 1982, they blessed 2,075 couples in Madison Square Garden, New York City; on October 14, 1982, they celebrated the marriage of 5,837 couples in Seoul. On October 20, 1988, there were 6,500 couples; on January 12, 1989, 1,275 couples. On August 25, 1992, the Unificationist marriage ceremony celebrated the "marriage" of 30,000 couples, of whom 20,000 were in the Olympic Stadium in Seoul, with another 10,000 in different parts of the planet, who followed the ceremony in Seoul transmitted by satellite in the presence of a representative of Rev. Moon who officiated in his place. This time an important proportion of the participating couples (70 percent, according to Unification sources) were not members of the church and had already married in another religious faith. By participating in the Unificationist ceremony, they hoped to reconsecrate their marriage, pledging to live as an ideal family as promoted by Rev. Moon. In 1994, when Rev. Moon established the Family Federation for World Peace and Unification, his idea was also to organize all blessed couples who are not members of the Unification Church.

Subsequent to the 1995 mass "blessing," there was a declaration that 3.6 million couples would be "blessed" in 1997. The main ceremony took place in John F. Kennedy Stadium in Washington, D.C., on November 29, 1997. The process of blessing on that occasion differed from previous blessings in two important aspects. First, any couple who had already received the blessing was allowed to officiate in blessing other couples, whereas previously it had been almost exclusively the position of the Reverend and Mrs. Moon to officiate. Second, the Holy Wine (or Nectar) and Holy Water Ceremony (traditionally not held on the same day as the blessing) could have been administered well in advance of the main ceremony. These "pre-blessings" of the Holy Wine and Holy Water ceremonies were subsequently completed by the Blessing Prayer of the Reverend and Mrs. Moon on November 29.

The 3.6 million couples' blessing was declared fulfilled on July 15, 1997, with an announcement that the blessing on November 29, 1997, would total 39.6 million couples. This blessing included a large proportion of couples from other faiths. The ceremony in Washington, D.C., included six "co-officiators" from other faiths, including controversial minister Louis Farrakhan from the Nation of Islam. The blessing ceremony in Seoul on February 7, 1999, featured seven co-officiators, including Orthodox rabbi Virgil Kranz (chair of the American Jewish Assembly), controversial Catholic archbishop Emmanuel Milingo, and the general superintendent of the Church of God in Christ (a large African-American Pentecostal denomination), Reverend T. L. Barrett.

On June 13, 1998, an earlier blessing ceremony centered in Madison Square Garden in New York City took place for 120 million couples worldwide. In the events center, more than 2,000 couples were joined together for the first time. These ceremonies culminated a campaign around the world to revive a "marriage culture." The majority of couples receiving the Reverend and Mrs. Moon's blessing were not Unificationists but had agreed to recommit to the following four vows:

1. To become a true man or woman who practices sexual purity and lives for the sake of others;

2. To become a true husband or wife who respects True Parents' example and establishes an eternal family which brings joy to God;

3. To become a parent who educates their children to

follow the tradition of true love for the sake of the family and world; and

4. To create an ideal family which contributes to world peace.

From June 13, 1998, to February 7, 1999, Unificationist sources claim that 240 million couples were "blessed." This, added to previous blessings, represented the earlier-than-expected fulfillment of the 360 million couples blessed during a three-year period which Rev. Moon had hoped to accomplish by 2000. The figures are disputed by critics and obviously difficult to verify. One way of reconciling the differences is to note that many thousands were given the Holy Wine and Holy Water at tables in public places without understanding the significance of the act. In Japan and other countries, giving out "holy candy" was also widely practiced. The majority of these people did not participate in formal blessing ceremonies, yet were probably counted by the church among the blessed.

The blessing in Seoul Olympic Stadium touched 40,000 couples. It was viewed in 185 different countries either by satellite or through the Internet. Some 150,000 couples were matched and blessed worldwide. For the first time, other elders of the church assisted the Reverend and Mrs. Moon.

The process of matching couples is increasingly being delegated by Reverend Moon to elder members of the movement. While Moon continues to match "second generation" couples (i.e., children of previous blessings), new "first generation" candidates are "pre-matched" by either National or Continental Blessing Committees composed of elder members or leaders who know the candidates personally. With the "Declaration of 9.9 Jeol," the "indemnity conditions" previously necessary to be blessed have been eliminated.

These conditions had included: fasting for seven days, "witnessing three spiritual children" (i.e., converting three new members), and having served a three-year mission.) After the "Declaration of 9.9 Jeol," the only remaining condition was a forty-day separation period before starting family life.

Besides the marriage blessing, the most solemn rite of the Unification Church is the "pledge"—a statement of dedication to establish the ideal family which is recited by families or members who come together at 5:00 a.m. every Sunday, as well as on the first day of the month and on certain holy days throughout the year. Unificationists celebrate a growing number of holy days with a 7:00 a.m. pledge service dressed in white "holy robes" before an "offering table" of fruits and foods which are offered to God and later consumed by the congregation. There are prayers and a sermon, and typically an entertainment event in the evening. The most important holy day is True God's Day each January 1. True Parents' Day, True Children's Day, and True Day of All Things are other holy days. Blessed families are expected to recite a special "Family Pledge" which in the latest version (revised in November 1998) contains the following words:

1. Our Family pledges to seek our original homeland and establish the original ideal of creation, the Kingdom of God on Earth and in Heaven, by centering on True Love.

2. Our Family pledges to represent and become central to Heaven and Earth by attending God and True Parents; We will perfect the dutiful way of filial piety in our family, patriotism in our nation, saints in the world, and divine sons and daughters in Heaven and Earth by centering on True Love.

3. Our Family pledges to perfect the Four Great Realms of Heart, the Three Great Kingships, the realm of the Royal Family, by centering on True Love

4. Our Family pledges to build the universal family encompassing Heaven and Earth, which is God's Ideal of creation, and perfect the world of freedom, peace, unity and happiness by centering on True Love.

5. Our Family pledges to strive every day to advance the unification of spirit world and physical world as subject and object partners, by centering on True Love.

6. Our Family pledges to embody God and True Parents; we will perfect a family which moves heavenly fortune and conveys Heaven's blessing to our community, by centering on True Love.

7. Our Family pledges to perfect a world based on the culture of heart, which is rooted in the original lineage, through living for the sake of others, by centering on True Love.

8. Our Family pledges, as we enter the Completed Testament Age, to achieve the ideal oneness of God and humankind in love through absolute faith, absolute love and absolute obedience, thereby perfecting the realm of liberation of the Kingdom of God on Earth and in Heaven, by centering on True Love.

On Sundays worship services are held. These consist of prayers, songs, a sermon, Bible readings, and/or readings from the *Divine Principle*. Other ceremonies may be organized during the week as well. On September 1, 1997, Rev. Moon declared the new tradition of *Hoon Dok Hae*, which entails, as mentioned earlier, reading excerpts (selected by him) of his speeches each morning between 6:00 and 7:00.

This activity has been aided by the publication of fifteen books, designed specifically for these daily study sessions, which collect excerpts from Rev. Moon's past speeches (which otherwise are collected sequentially in more than 230 books) on specific topics.

In Unification Church worship, an important position is given to the photograph of the True Parents, Rev. Moon and his wife, often accompanied by one or more of their children. Rev. Moon has advised members to carry on their person a photograph of the True Parents. Such photographs are normally placed in every center and in every Unification home and are also present inside places of worship. Traditionally, all "blessed" members concluded their prayers "in the holy names of True Parents. Amen." However, Reverend Moon on September 14, 1999, instructed them to conclude in their own names as "a blessed family that has inherited True Parents' realm of victory through the blessing. Amen." Unification Church members have also been advised to place a Unification Church flag outside their houses or a sticker on their door. Theologically, this has a significance similar to the blood placed on doors of Jews at the time of the Passover in Egypt. (The same theological significance has been invoked for other deeds, from distributing copies of the *Divine Principle* to giving out Holy Wine).

After the untimely death by a car accident in 1984 of one of Rev. Moon's children, seventeen-year-old Heung Jin Nim, a strong movement of sympathy began in the church for this young man to whom had been attributed the role of mediator between the spirit world and our world (in this sense he was called a "young Christ"). Certain Unificationists—such as Faith Jones in England and Clophas Kundioni in Zimbabwe—received during the 1980s revelations from Heung Jin Nim.[3] The young man from Zimbabwe was at one time considered to be "the second personality of Heung Jin Nim." Kundioni led a controversial repentance and revival movement within the church for a short time in 1987-88. Jones's and Kundioni's roles ended at the end of the 1980s. The repentance movement was accompanied by Rev. Moon's request that all "blessed members" repent in prayer prior to drinking Holy Water in late 1987.

Besides the photograph of the True Parents, the church insists on either (preferably) using holy salt or blowing three times after a formula prayer to purify things from the material world (but not people) and thus remove them from Satan's dominion. There is also the consecration of "holy grounds" (the one in France, for example, is found in the Field of Martyrs in Paris; another is in St. Peter's Square in Rome, at the entrance to Vatican City). Also, different types of candles may be used as sacred objects in the Unification Church, as well as "Holy Robes" worn by blessed family members during ceremonies or on particular Holy Days.

The Unification Church does not practice formal baptism, although the sprinkling of Holy Water during blessings is sometimes explained in this way. However, the church does provide a "birth ceremony." Following the birth of a child, seven "birth candles" are lit and three "blessed wives" pray simultaneously, preferably in the same room where the birth took place or, if this is not possible, in another room. Eight days after the birth, the child is offered up to God, in a prayerful ceremony, by its parents and their friends.

The funeral ceremony for "blessed members" is called the *Seung Wha* ceremony. This was installed after the death of Rev. Moon's son, Heung Jin Moon, in January 1984. The church explains that originally the _Seung Wha_ ceremony should not have been initiated until the True Parents had first passed into the spiritual world. Then they could have received their children and disciples by the _Seung Wha_ ceremony. Nevertheless, because of Heung Jin Moon's devotion and his work in the spiritual world, blessed members may receive the foundation of the _Seung Wha_ ceremony.

The _Seung Wha_ ceremony is "joyful" because it celebrates the beginning of new life as a purely spiritual being. For women, black must not be worn during the ceremony, only white and pastels. Men wear white holy robes, if possible, or at least suits with white ties. At the cemetery there is a shorter service (_Won Jeun_) which is made up of a song, a prayer, a short sermon, and the covering of the lowered casket with flowers. There are other ceremonies which take place when the cemetery is visited again and at the home where the deceased once lived. These funeral ceremonies are reserved for blessed members only, those united in matrimony by the True Parents, or their children. The same rituals are not given to unmarried members; the funeral rituals for such members have not yet been formulated. Nevertheless, unmarried members are assured that they too will enjoy a good place in the spiritual world, even if they did not receive the marriage blessing. There has been, however, some recent confusion among church members, since Mrs. Hyo Nam Kim in Chung Pyung teaches that the influence of evil spirits is so prevalent that even blessed members may be dragged down to hell unless they receive the liberation dispensed by Dae Mo Nim (the spirit of Mrs. Moon's mother).

5.

Controversies

Rev. Moon often presents his doctrine (as the name of his church indicates) as an instrument for "the unification of World Christianity" and to eliminate divisions among Christians and world religions in general. Some people take this declaration seriously and consider Unificationism as a useful viewpoint regarding ecumenism to promote Christian unity. Numerous young adherents to the Unification Church in the early years, who came from the Catholic church (and were interviewed by Jesuit sociologist Joseph Fichter), declared: "Today I am a better Catholic than before," believing they had not left the Catholic church, but instead had learned to develop more completely the virtues and practices of Catholicism.[1] Today it is clear that Unificationism presents a theology that is very different from Catholic or mainline Protestant theology. Unificationism is not a new "viewpoint" with regard to Christianity, nor is it a simple instrument made available for ecumenism. Unificationism is a new religion, one that differs from both Catholicism and mainline Protestantism.

We may ask ourselves why the Unification Church—whose theology and activities are not very different from other messianic and communal groups—has caused so much more controversy than other movements. Three reasons can be identified, two of which are now obsolete but continue to be repeated (particularly in Europe) by the anticult movement, which seems not to understand that such movements move and change their historical attitudes. The first reason for hostility relates to the church's missionary style, especially that practiced by the Oakland Family in California: not immediately identifying the missionary as being affiliated with the Unification Church, followed by a tendency to isolate converted young people from their original families. In this case, the Unification Church has unquestionably committed mistakes—the hostile attitudes of some families and the practice of "deprogramming" did not help matters—but these are problems that for the most part no longer exist, at least from the 1980s on.

It is within this context that accusations of "brainwashing" were often accepted by the press, even if theories of "brainwashing" in general have been rejected by most academic scholars of new religious movements. Certain missionary techniques of the Unification Church are, in fact, quite sophisticated, but—as mentioned earlier—they are not irresistible, because the numbers show that the percentage of people who join is never more than 10 percent of those who participate in the church's seminars. Contrary to what certain "apostate" ex-members maintain, scholarly and law enforcement enquiries have consistently concluded that no Unificationist has ever been held against his or her will, nor been restricted from moving around freely or leaving the church if so desired. Every year a number of people leave the church spontaneously while others join. This is common in new religious movements.

Second, the Unification Church has been attacked especially in the 1970s and 1980s for its anti-Communist political activities. It has been accused of confusing religion and politics and of using the religious enthusiasm of its disciples and the donations received for political purposes. The church has systematically denied these accusations and maintained that the donations are used solely for religious activities, while the funds used for sustaining journalistic, cultural, or political activities come from the movement's commercial enterprises and from its financial investments. However, the anti-Communism of the Unification Church was not only political but is embodied in its world vision and its history of theology. Naturally, after 1989, anti-Communism no longer has a central role in the church.

The controversies regarding the Unification Church should reasonably have diminished in the 1990s, a period during which the church's proselyting techniques greatly changed, many members were no longer full time, and the anti-Communist controversy was superseded by other concerns and interests. This mitigation of controversy happened to some degree in the United States and in Korea (where newspapers founded by Rev. Moon, the *Washington Times* and the *Sae Gye Ilbo*, are now considered part of the mainline press), but not in Europe or Japan. The Unification Church in Europe was involved in the resurgence of anti-cult campaigns which followed the murders/suicides of the Order of the Solar Temple (1994-97), and both Rev. Moon and his wife have been denied entry into some countries on the basis of lists compiled under the Schengen Agreement, a measure which seems to seriously contradict the principles of personal and religious freedoms.

From a different perspective, it is true that participation of people who are not members of the Unification Church in certain Unificationist activities, such as marriage blessings, may be of some concern to established churches.

They perceive the possibility that their own members may become confused by their participation in such Unificationist activities and fear that they may in fact end up converting to Unificationism. Sociological studies demonstrate that this is unlikely, that participation in Unificationist activities (including the blessings) only rarely cause non-Unificationists to convert to the Unification Church. On the other hand, a serious study of the theology of the Unification Church should make it impossible for any confusion to occur: it is an original and specific theology, and dual membership in the Unification Church and another church—for example, the Catholic or Baptist church— should logically be excluded.

There is yet another reason for the enduring controversy. While participation in a Christian church for most people is limited to one hour on Sundays, the Unification Church asks of its members, even when they are not full time, a more demanding degree of participation. To be a member of the Unification Church is not only a way of spending Sundays, but something which becomes the primary distinctive character of a member's identity. The secular anti-cult movements do not accept that the identity of a person who is not a member of the clergy could be primarily defined according to his or her religious obligation, particularly when this obligation is severe and strict. For those who take such an anti-cult stance, this identity is incompatible with modernity itself, and must be the result of some form of brainwashing or mind control. The problem at this point, however, goes beyond the case of Unificationism. In a post-modern world, where the tenets of modernity (secularization included) are called into question, the cult/anti-cult controversy will probably be transformed by the use of new arguments or simply become obsolete.

Notes

CHAPTER 1. SOURCES

1. The Unification Church throughout the English-speaking world has used for many years the *Divine Principle* in its "5th edition" (in fact, the fourth printing of the second edition), published in New York by the Holy Spirit Association for the Unification of World Christianity, 1972. The original is in Korean and there exist official translations only in Japanese, English, and Spanish (an official translation in Italian, 1976, is no longer in circulation, but a new translation is forthcoming). A new official translation from Korean to English was completed in 1996 by a committee including two sons of the late original editor, Rev. Hyo Won Eu: *Exposition of the Divine Principle* (New York: The Holy Spirit Association for the Unification of World Christianity). A summary for beginners in studying the Divine Principle is entitled *Outline of the Principles: Level 4* (New York: The Holy Spirit Association for the Unification of World Christianity, 1980).

2. Jin-choon Kim, "A Study of the Formation and History of the Unification Principle," *Journal of Unification Studies* 2 (1998): 49-69.

3. See *The Sermons of the Reverend Sun Myung Moon*; there are currently 236 volumes, dating back to 1956, in Korean (with titles in English as well). Only the first seven volumes are translated into English (see *Sermons of Rev. Sun Myung Moon* [New York: The Holy Spirit Association for the Unification of World Christianity, 1994]). In 1986 the Holy Spirit Association for the Unification of World Christianity, New York, published a book

entitled *Reverend Moon Speaks from Prison* which includes seven talks by Rev. Moon revised by the author during his first months in the American prison at Danbury.

4. See Young Oon Kim, *Unification Theology* (New York: The Holy Spirit Association for the Unification of World Christianity, 1987).

5. Sang Hun Lee, *Explaining Unification Thought* (New York: Unification Thought Institute, 1981).

6. See *The End of Communism* (New York: Unification Thought Institute, 1985); in fact, this volume completed, and replaced, a previous work on the same argument entitled *Communism—A Critique & Counter Proposal* (Washington, D.C.: The Freedom Leadership Foundation, 1973).

7. Sang Hun Lee, *Life in the Spirit World and on Earth*, recorded by Young Soon Kim (New York: Family Federation for World Peace and Unification, 1998).

8. Andrew Wilson, "Visions of the Spirit World: Sang Hun Lee's 'Life in the Spirit World and on Earth' Compared with Other Spiritualist Accounts," *Journal of Unification Studies* 2 (1998): 123-47 (123).

9. See Mose Durst, *To Bigotry No Sanction: Reverend Sun Myung Moon and the Unification Church* (Chicago: Regnery Gateway, 1984). On the legal problems in the United States, see also John T. Biermans, *The Odyssey of New Religions Today: A Case Study of the Unification Church,* 2nd ed. (Lewiston, NY: The Edwin Mellen Press, 1988).

10. See *The Sun Rising in the Shade. The Autobiography of Chong Goo (Tiger) Park* (New York: Collegiate Association for the Research of the Principle, 1989).

11. See Henri Blanchard, *Au Nom de l'amour vrai* [In the Name of True Love] (Paris: A.E.S.U.C.M., 1985).

12. For the rituals, see *The Tradition: Book One* (New York: The Holy Spirit Association for the Unification of World Christianity, 1985).

13. Michael Breen, *Sun Myung Moon: The Early Years, 1920-53* (Hurstpierpoint, West Sussex: Refuge Books, 1997).

14. See John Lofland, *Doomsday Cult* (Englewood Cliffs, NJ: Prentice-Hall, 1966). Even in the second edition (subtitled *A*

Study of Conversion, Proselytism and Maintainance of Faith [New York: Irvington, 1977]), Lofland did not want to abandon the pseudonyms used in the first (for example, the *Divine Principle* is called the *Divine Precepts,* Rev. Moon is called Mr. Chang, and so on).

15. See Eileen Barker, *The Making of a Moonie: Choice or Brainwashing?* (Oxford: Basil Blackwell, 1984).

16. See David G. Bromley and Anson D. Shupe, Jr., *"Moonies" in America: Cult, Church and Crusade* (Beverly Hills, CA: Sage, 1979).

17. See George D. Chryssides, *The Advent of Sun Myung Moon: The Origins, Beliefs and Practices of the Unification Church* (London: Macmillan, 1991).

18. See Joseph H. Fichter, "Marriage, Family and Sun Myung Moon," *America,* October 27, 1979, 226-28. See also by the same author, *The Holy Family of Father Moon* (Kansas City: Leaven, 1985).

19. See, for example, on the presence of women in the movement, Kathleen S. Lowney, *Passport to Heaven: Gender Roles in the Unification Church* (New York, 1992).

20. See Sebastian A. Matczak, *Unificationism: A New Philosophy and Worldview* (Jamaica, NY: Learned Publications, 1982).

21. See, for example, Bryan Wilson, ed., *The Social Impact of New Religious Movements* (New York: Rose of Sharon Press, 1981), published following a conference organized by the Unification Theological Seminary in Barrytown; see also a work by a member of the Unification Church, sociologist Michael L. Mickler, *A History of the Unification Church in America, 1959-1974: Emergence of a National Movement* (New York: Garland, 1993).

22. See Deanna Durham, *Life Among the Moonies: Three Years in the Unification Church* (Plainfield: Logos International, 1981).

23. Nansook Hong, *In The Shadow of the Moons: My Life in Reverend Sun Myung Moon's Family* (Boston: Little, Brown & Company, 1998).

24. Among the most notable early works are those by James Bjornstadt, *The Moon Is Not the Sun* (Minneapolis: Dimension Books, 1976), and J. Isamu Yamamoto, *The Puppet Master* (Downers Grove, IL: InterVarsity Press, 1977).

25. See Pierre Le Cabellec, "Moon or Jesus," *Bulletin Interparoissial de Lorient*, April 3, 1977; and *Dossier Moon* (Mullhouse: Salvator, 1983).

26. Cf. Jean-François Boyer, *L'Empire Moon* (Paris: La Decouverte, 1986).

27. See bibliography in *The Brainwashing/Deprogramming Controversy: Sociological, Psychological, Legal and Historical Perspectives,* edited by D. G. Bromley and James T. Richardson (New York: Edwin Mellen, 1983). For a legal approach, see Thomas Robbins, William C. Sheperd, and James McBride, eds., *Cults, Culture and the Law: Perspectives on New Religious Movements* (Chicago: Scholar Press, 1985).

28. See Ted Patrick, with Tom Dulack, *Let Our Children Go!* (New York: Ballantine, 1976).

29. See A. D. Shupe, Jr., D. G. Bromley, and Donna L. Oliver, *The Anti-Cult Movement in America: A Bibliography and Historical Survey* (New York: Garland, 1984); J. Gordon Melton, *The Modern Anti-Cult Movement in Historical Perspective* (Santa Barbara, CA: The Institute for the Study of American Religion, 1995).

CHAPTER 2. HISTORY

1. See also Frederick Sontag, *Sun Myung Moon and the Unification Church* (Nashville: Abingdon, 1977).

2. See Breen, 62.

3. Going to North Korea and the difficult relationship with Mrs. Sun Kil Choi are described in Rev. Moon's autobiographical speech "The Path for Our Family," Chung Pyung Training Center, August 28, 1971, in the section "You can't expect to have a father/son relationship without walking the miserable path" (available from http://www.tparents.org/library/moon/talks/moon71/UM710828.htm).

4. See Breen, 154-59.

5. This refers to the marriage ceremony of the Unification Church. It is claimed that through this ceremony Original Sin is forgiven and couples are removed from Satan's blood lineage and are grafted into God's blood lineage. Only Rev. and Mrs. Moon officiated in Blessing Ceremonies until 1995 (see chap. 4).

6. See W. P. Kim, *Father's Course and Our Life of Faith* (London: The Holy Spirit Association for the Unification of World Christianity, 1982); the author is one of the oldest disciples of Rev. Moon.

7. Chung Hwa Pak, one of Rev. Moon's first disciples, caused considerable controversy by confirming these accusations in a text widely circulated by critics (and later published in Japanese) called *The Tragedy of the Six Marys*. Pak, who had left the Unification Church, claimed that Rev. Moon practiced during the church's early years sex rituals with, among others, six married female disciples ("the six Marys") who were to have prepared the way for the virgin who would marry him and become the True Mother. The church vehemently denied the allegations. Pak eventually returned to the fold and, shortly before dying, recanted all the accusations in a second text he authored in 1995, called *The Apostate*. Similar accusations were discussed earlier in libel cases in Korea and not proved. In 1989, after a ten-year legal case, the Seoul District Criminal Court (79 ko dan 3372) convicted a protestant minister, Rev. Shin Sa-hun, of criminal libel after his accusations of sexual misconduct could not be proved. In another case decided by the Seoul District Civil Court (83 ga hap 3012), damages were paid by Tak Myung-hwan, a well-known critic of the Unification Church, to a woman who had been accused of having an illegitimate son with Rev. Moon and to her son. Corrections were published by the Christian newspapers *Gidok Shinbo* on October 8, 1983, and *Hankook Gidok Gongbo*, on October 1, 1983, after printing similar accusations of sexual misconduct in the early Unification Church. Part of the retraction stated, "The article 'The Secret Sexual Practices of the Unification Religion' was a repetition of information published during the 1950s, and we have found it to have no basis in fact."

8. See Ken Sudo, *The 120-Day Training Manual* (Belvedere, NY: The Holy Spirit Association for the Unification of World Christianity, 1975).

9. There are other newspapers: in Japan, *Sekai Nippo*, beginning in 1975; in Cairo, *Middle East Times*; in South Korea, *Sae Gye Ilbo*, beginning in 1989; in Uruguay, *Ultimas Noticias*; and a

pan-Latin American newspaper, *Tiempos del Mundo*, established in Buenos Aires in 1996.

10. See Bo Hi Pak, *A Historic Defence: Before the U.S. Congress Subcommitee* (London: Unification Church, 1978).

11. Transcript of Statements Made in the House of Commons, February 3, 1988, 3:30 p.m., p. 978.

12. See *World Scriptures: A Comparative Anthology of Sacred Texts: A Project of the International Religious Foundation* (New York: Paragon House, 1991).

13. John McClaughry, "Pyrrhic Victory Over Moon," *New York Times*, May 20, 1984.

14. William Rapsberry, "A Fair Trial for Rev. Moon," *Washington Post*, April 18, 1984.

15. During a visit to Paris in 1992, Mrs. Moon expressed her surprise that any French Unificationists were still associated with the National Front. This led to a severing of remaining ties.

16. The University of Bridgeport was rescued from severe financial troubles by the Professors World Peace Academy (PWPA) in 1992 in return for majority shareholding. Since then $100 million has been spent on the University of Bridgeport (see "Group tied to Unification Church gives another $3.5 million to BU," Associated Press, April 6, 1999). PWPA is funded by the International Cultural Foundation (ICF) which was established by Rev. Moon to promote academic, scientific, and cultural activities. According to Rev. Moon's projects, the University of Bridgeport should become an important component, together with the Sun Moon University in South Korea, of the proposed World University Foundation. This is conceived as a network of universities which will allow students to study at several universities either by distance learning or by changing their residency. Another project initiated at the University of Bridgeport, on November 21, 1998, is the Health and Science Centre whose aim is to incorporate all types of Eastern and Western medicine, both orthodox and alternative, in one institution.

17. Alex Bellos, "Moon's Last Stand," *Guardian's Saturday Review* (London), September 26, 1998.

18. For details of this new repentance movement, see "Understanding Dae Mo Nim's Earthly Activity at Chung Pyung from

the Viewpoint of Divine Principle," by Dr. Chang Shik Yang, director of Unification Church's Mid-Atlantic Region, USA, March 1998 (http://www.tparents.org/Library/Unification/Talks/Yang/O-Toc.htm#TableofContents).

19. A. Wilson, 23.

20. Hong.

21. See HSA-UWC North America Family Church, "Questions and Answers About Nan Sook Hong's Book," by Rev. Joong Hyun Pak, Continental Director, and Dr. Tyler Hendricks, President, October 3, 1998.

22. Rev. Sun Myung Moon, "Inaugural Address," February 6, 1999, Lotte Hotel, Seoul, Korea.

CHAPTER 3. DOCTRINE

1. *Exposition of the Divine Principle*, 7.

2. Ibid., 104-105.

3. Ibid., 7.

4. Ibid., 108.

5. See *Introduction to the Principle: An Islamic Perspective* (New York: The Holy Spirit Association for the Unification of World Christianity, 1980).

6. Rev. Sun Myung Moon, "The Meaning of the Day of Victory of Love," January 2, 1997, Sao Paulo, Brazil; "True Parents' Day Is My True Son's Day," April 18, 1996, World Mission Center, New York.

7. That is, his own half-sister. Rev. Moon has referred in this respect to the fact Adam and Eve were "brother and sister." He insists that the Unification Church does not condone incest, but for key providential families there are actions required to fulfill the Providence of Restoration that seem to violate normal human standards.

8. *Exposition of Divine Principle*, 167.

9. This reinterpretation of the role of biblical personages opens the way to possible schisms, as when a dissident decides to reinterpret the role of Rev. Moon himself. In this way, Myong-Sok Jong, a Korean who made his disciples call him "Jesus Morning Star," has accused Rev. Moon of committing the

same error as John the Baptist, by not recognizing his role as a simple forerunner to the authentic messianic figure—i.e., Jong himself. The Church of the Providence founded by Jong has around 30,000 follwers and is controverial in Korea because of the importance he attributes to soccer as a means of spiritual elevation for men and because of a devotion ritual to the founder in which, according to critics, some of the female disciples offer their bodies to him. On the Church of the Providence, see the work of French anti-cult ethnologist Nathalie Luca, *Le Salut par le foot. Une ethnologue chez un messie coréen* (Geneva: Labor et Fides, 1997).

CHAPTER 4. SPIRITUALITY AND MISSIONARY ACTIVITIES

1. Bromley and Shupe, 122-23.

2. See E. Barker, 105.

3. Nim is a Korean word of respect. Heung Jin Moon is often respectfully called "Heung Jin Nim" by Unificationists.

CHAPTER 5. CONTROVERSIES

1. See Fichter, *The Holy Family of Father Moon*, 25.

Bibliographical Note

Among the most important scholarly studies of the Unification movement are: David G. Bromley and Anson D. Shupe, *"Moonies" in America: Cult, Church and Crusade* (Beverly Hills, CA: Sage, 1979); Joseph H. Fichter, *The Holy Family of Father Moon* (Kansas City, MO: Leaven, 1985); Eileen Barker, *The Making of a Moonie: Choice or Brainwashing?* (Oxford, Eng.: Basil Blackwell, 1984); and George D. Chryssides, *The Advent of Sun Myung Moon: The Origins, Beliefs and Practices of the Unification Church* (London: Macmillan, 1991). There is also an important article in Italian by Eileen Barker: "La rivelazione della Chiesa dell'Unificazione del reverendo Moon," in M. Introvigne, ed., *Le nuove rivelazioni* (Leumann: Elle Di Ci, 1991), pp. 123-43.

About the Author and Series Editor

Massimo Introvigne was born in Rome and is the managing director of the Center for Studies on New Religions (CESNUR), a network of international academic organizations devoted to the study of emerging religious/spiritual movements. An attorney in private practice in Torino, Italy, he has taught courses and seminars in several academic institutions on the sociology and history of new religions. Additionally, he is the author or editor of some forty books and numerous articles and chapters on the same topic.